Ochre Peak Publishing Limited

Vanderhoof, British Columbia

No part of this publication may be reproduced, stored in retrieval system, or transmitted in any form, or by any means, electronic, mechanical, photocopying, recording, or otherwise, without written permission of the publisher. For information regarding permission, write to Ochre Peak Publishing, 12538 Highway 27, Vanderhoof, British Columbia, Canada, V0J 3A2.

ISBN 978-1-7382476-0-8

Text copyright 2024 by A. MacDonal-Geddes. Illustration copyright 2024 by Roka Studio. All rights reserved.

Published by Ochre Peak Publishing Limited, 12538 Highway 27, Vanderhoof, British Columbia, V0J 3A2

The publisher does not have any control over and does not assume any responsiblity for author or third-party

Rob loved being safe. He wanted everyone and everything near him to be safe too.

When Rob walked through town, he made sure there was nothing to trip over. He looked for kittens in trees. He even helped people cross the street.

Rob felt safety was so important that he got a job as a safety officer. What a lucky man he was! Now he could spend every day keeping people safe.

"I love my job!" he said happily.

Rob got to drive a shiny orange truck with the words "Safety Rob" on the door.

His new boss asked him to drive around town and make sure all the traffic lights were working.

"I'm on it!" he smiled.

As Safety Rob started to drive, the boss called out, "Be safe, Rob! And always wear your seatbelt!"

At the end of a busy first day, Safety Rob drove home. He used his turn signals and stopped at red lights. Rob sat in his driveway and smiled. Then he looked at the empty seat beside him.

"I wish I had a safety partner to work with every day."

Rob thought about a safety partner while he ate his supper. After safely washing the dishes, in water which was not too hot, he decided to sew a new safety vest.

"If I get a partner, they can wear this vest."

Rob was very safe while he made the vest. He used his scissors safely and was careful not to poke himself with the pointy end of the needle.

When it was done, Safety Rob held up the vest.

"I guess I had less fabric than I thought. I'm going to need a very small partner."

Safety Rob went to bed, knowing he was always extra safe after a good night's sleep.

In the morning, Safety Rob put on his own orange safety vest, picked up the small vest, and headed out the door.

Rob was so busy thinking about a partner, he forgot to pay attention and tripped on the top step. He hit the ground with a bounce.

"That wasn't safe," he groaned. Suddenly, something wet slapped his hand. It was the tongue of a brown and white shaggy dog.

Safety Rob leaned over to look at the dog, and the little orange safety vest dropped over its head. The dog danced in excitement and wiggled its way right into the vest.

"Now, don't you look safe!" smiled Rob.

The dog sat on the ground beside Safety Rob. "Ranger Dog" was written on a bone-shaped name tag.

"Where did you come from, Ranger Dog?" asked Safety Rob trying to pull the vest back over the dog's head.

Ranger Dog growled.

"Always be careful around dogs," Safety Rob reminded himself. "Especially dogs you don't know."

Safety Rob stood. Ranger Dog stood. Safety Rob walked ten steps toward the truck. So did the dog.

Safety Rob opened the door and the dog jumped in. Rob climbed into the truck and put on his seatbelt.

"I'm late for work. You'll have to spend the day with me. We will find your owners this evening."

Before driving, Safety Rob phoned his boss to tell her he was on his way. Then he put his phone away.

"Out of sight, out of mind!" he said as he started down the road. "Never use your phone while driving."

As they safely arrived at work, the boss came over with a piece of paper.

"Here is your list of safety jobs, Rob. It's a long list."

Safety Rob took the paper and started to read. Ranger Dog looked at the list and appeared to read along.

"This is my friend, Ranger Dog, and we will get the jobs done!"

"Woof!" said Ranger Dog.

"Excellent!" said the boss and she patted Ranger Dog on the head and gave him a treat."

Rob looked at the list. "Help Farmer Tom move his cows safely." Safety Rob scratched his head

"How do we find Farmer Tom?" The boss handed them a map. "Excellent!" said Safety Rob.

Safety Rob looked at the map, handed it to Ranger Dog, and started to drive.

He waved at the boss. She waved back. Then she waved again. The third time she waved, she jumped up and down and waved both arms.

"What a friendly boss."

Suddenly Rob stopped.

"Where did the road go?"

They could see the boss running toward them. She was still waving. Rob waved again.

"You went the wrong way," the boss panted as she reached the truck.

Ranger Dog picked up the map in his paws, looked at it, and turned it around.

"It was upside down. We went the wrong way," said Safety Rob.

"Reading maps the right way keeps you safe," said the boss.

"I have something for you," said the boss and she handed Safety Rob another piece of paper.

On the paper was written:

"Ranger Dog does not have a family. He will be your safety partner."

Rob started to drive. His new safety partner, Ranger Dog, sat happily beside him.

"Off to Farmer Tom's we go!!"

Safety Rob smiled, "This will be so much fun!"

"Woof!"

In book 2, *Safety Rob and Ranger Dog: On the Farm*, the safety partners spend the day with Farmer Tom and his animals. They help move cows, learn all about tractor safety, and even spend some time in the farmhouse kitchen cooking a meal and baking pies.

Available summer, 2024.